RED LIGHT, GREEN LIGHT

SCHOLASTIC HARDCOVER is a registered trademark of Scholastic Inc.

Library of Congress Cataloging-in-Publication Data

Brown, Margaret Wise, 1910-1952.
Red light, green light/by Margaret Wise Brown: illustrated by Leonard Weisgard.
p.   cm.
Summary: All day and night the traffic signal blinks its messages of stop and go.
ISBN 0-590-44558-8
1. Traffic signs and signals—Fiction. I. Weisgard, Leonard, 1916-   ill. II. Title.
PZ7.B8163Re   1992
[E]—dc20   91-14589
                                                                        CIP
                                                                        AC

12 11 10 9 8 7 6 5 4 3 2 1   1 2 3 4 5 6/9

Printed in Mexico.   36

First Scholastic printing, May 1992

Book design by Laurie McBarnette

The artwork for this book was done in mixed media technique including the use of
casein, watercolor, crayon, and ink.

RED LIGHT, GREEN LIGHT

Written by Margaret Wise Brown

Illustrated by Leonard Weisgard

SCHOLASTIC
HARDCOVER

SCHOLASTIC INC.

New York

RED LIGHT

GREEN LIGHT

GOOD MORNING

STOP

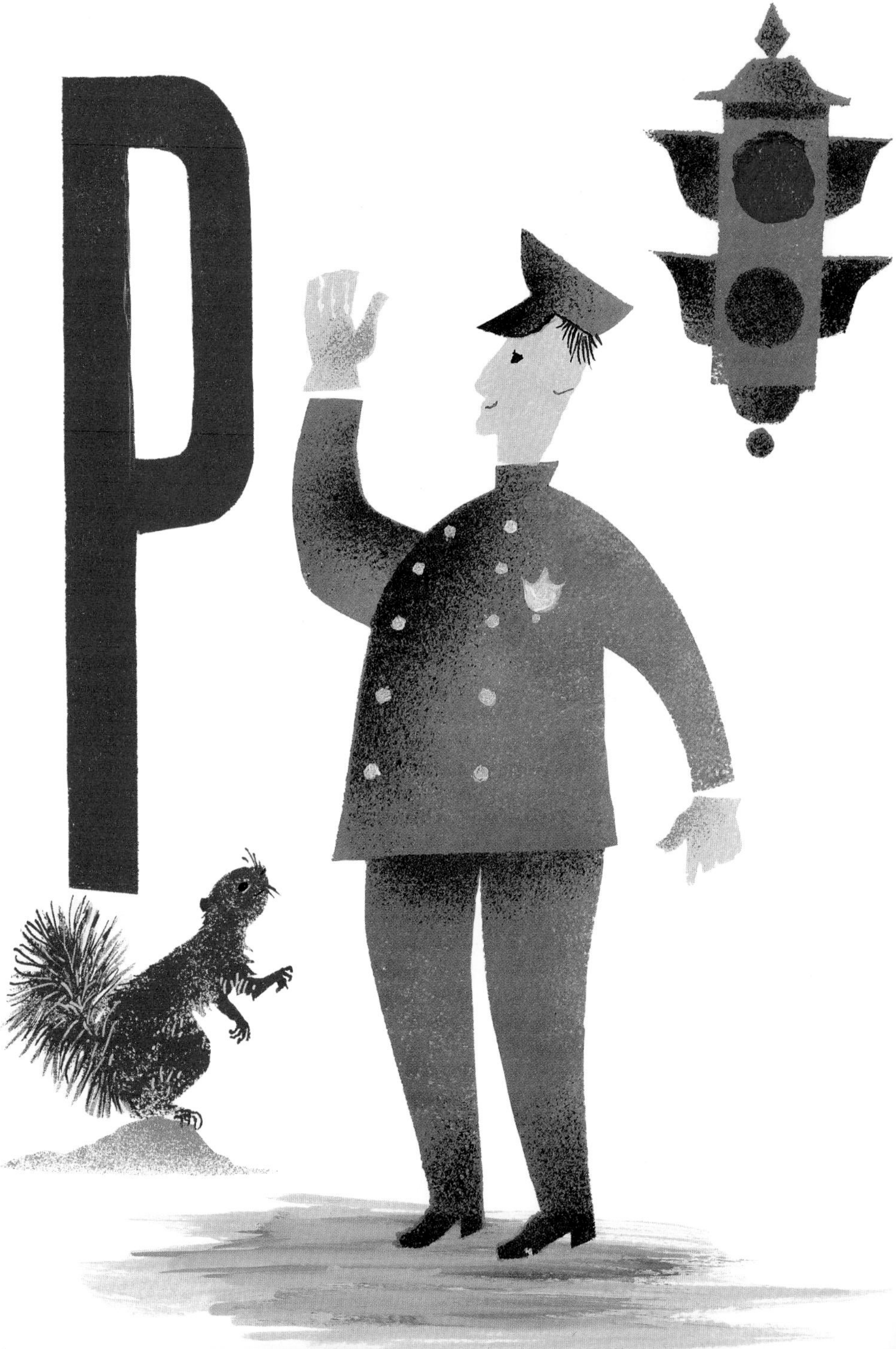

In the morning they all came out of their houses.

Red Light they can't go.

Green Light they can go.

The truck came out of the truck's house

a garage.

The car came out of the car's house

another garage.

The jeep came out of the jeep's house

a tent.

The horse came out of the horse's house

a barn.

The boy came out of the boy's house

a *home*.

The dog came out of the dog's house

a *kennel*.

The cat climbed down from the cat's house

a *tree*.

(This was a wild cat.)

And the mouse came out of the house of the mouse

a *hole*.

Red Light they can't go.

Green Light they can.

And they all went down
their own roads.

Truck and car and bicycle
and horse roads

Jeep roads across fields

Dog roads

Cat roads

And mouse roads through the grass.

Green Light they can go.

Red Light they can't.

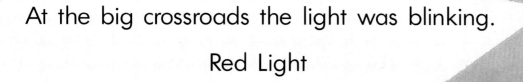

At the big crossroads the light was blinking.

Red Light

The truck comes roaring along.

Red Light

Stop.

The car comes whizzing along.

Red Light

Stop.

The jeep comes jeeping along.

Red Light

Stop.

The horse comes trotting along.

Red Light

Stop.

The cat comes creeping along.

Red Light

Stop.

RED LIGHT

The mouse came along.

Red Light a bunny's eyes.

Green Light a cat's.

STOP

GREEN LIGHT

Green Light they did go.

Red Light they didn't.

They went around all day until it was night.

Then all the lights turned on along the
roads and in the houses because it was night.
And they all went home.

Red Light they didn't go.
Green Light they did.

The truck went into the truck's house

a garage.

The car went into the car's house

another garage.

The jeep went into the jeep's house

a tent.

The horse went into the horse's house

a barn.

The boy went into the boy's house

a *home.*

The dog went into the dog's house

a *kennel.*

The cat went into the cat's house

a *tree.*

(This was a wild cat.)

And the mouse crept into the house of the mouse

a *hole.*

Red Light they can't go.

Green Light they can.

All things were asleep.

Through holes and doors and windows

lights blinked off

until there was only a Red Light

and a Green Light

blinking in the darkness.

RED LIGHT

GREEN LIGHT

GOOD NIGHT

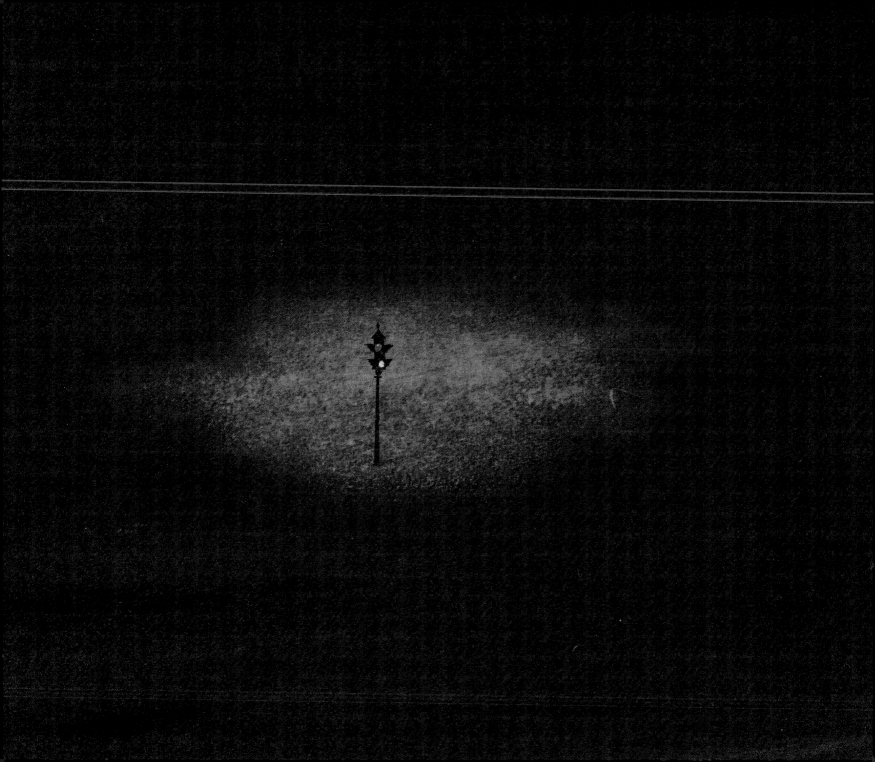